I0426013

Assisted Living

Emergency Move Assistant


by

Jerrod Ayers, ALM/MBA

and

Nicole Walker, LPN


Copyright © 2013 J.P. Ayers

Please contact the author at jpayersbooks@gmail.com
for corporate rates.

# Introduction

## What is the purpose of this book?

If you are reading this, likely your interest in Assisted Living (AL) is not limited to curiosity. You are a senior who is in a position that Assisted Living may be a necessity, or a convenience. You could be the loved one of a senior that has presented with a need. Perhaps a physician or other healthcare professional has recommended a "nursing home" and after some quick research you've been left overwhelmed with your head throbbing and a knot in your stomach.

You are faced with understanding the behemoth known as our healthcare system and navigating the murky waters of determining the right place. This is not limited to just which company has better programs or a better reputation, but which type of healthcare facility is appropriate. The extreme cost of a care facility can range from state covered programs to well over $10,000 per month!

My intent with this book is to share my experience in the field with you in the hope that it will assist in making the appropriate decision for the person in need *and* the family. I could easily bombard you, the reader, with a 500 page manual that explains even the most mundane aspects of long term care. I do not think it is necessary, nor prudent to concoct such a document. This book is intended to be read quickly and used as a guide to both understanding the vocabulary and concepts common throughout the industry, as well as provide an overview of Long Term Care. At the end of the book are two forms which may be photocopied and used to aid in comparing facilities and making the best decision.

I have worked primarily in Arizona, so the information is presented based upon Arizona standards, practices and laws.

In my experience, quite often the need for a Long Term Care facility has arisen from a "trigger event" and time is of the essence. As a result, a huge majority of AL move-ins can be regarded as an emergency, or at least as an urgent move-in. Often the adult children are forced to put their own busy lives on hold and find a place for mom or dad after something has happened. Perhaps they are confined to a hospital after a recent illness, injury or diagnosis of a new condition. This makes the process that much more stressful.

I will discuss the different types of facilities in Long Term Care and the disadvantages and advantages of each format, how to partner with your prospective resident, some resources that may assist in affording a facility, and what to expect before, during and after the move.

I hope this will help dispel some myths surrounding the industry and provide you with the ability to take a more confident, informed approach to a huge decision.

# Table of Contents

5

# Chapter 1

## A brief introduction to Long Term Care

The first topic is intended to orient you to the industry specific terminology you'll hear thrown around, available levels of care and how they all fit together. This should help focus your search and allow you to understand some of the essential players in the process.

### Terminology

**AL:** Assisted Living

**IL:** Independent Living

**MC:** Memory Care/Alzheimer

**SNF:** Skilled Nursing Facility or Rehabilitation Facility.

**Activities of Daily Living (ADL's):** Assistance with one or more of these is the core of Assisted Living. The activities of daily living are daily tasks required to maintain a healthy lifestyle. They are:

> Personal Hygiene and Grooming
>
> Dressing
>
> Continence Care (toileting)
>
> Dining
>
> Transferring and Ambulation
>
> Medication Management
>
> Bathing/Showering

**Administrator or Licensed Nursing Home Administrator (LNHA):** In most states, there is a licensing difference between an Licensed Nursing Home Administrator and an Assisted Living Manager. An Administrator generally requires more education and a licensed Administrator is required to manage a SNF.

**Assisted Living Manager (ALM):** A certified or licensed manager that is responsible for overall operations of an AL or MC. Some companies refer to any facility manager as an "Administrator", but in most states an AL requires an ALM licensee even if the manager is already a LNHA.

**Behavioral Health:** A facility that specializes in caring for individuals with behavioral problems and provides psychiatric treatment.

**Community:** The industry term for a facility. The goal is to differentiate from a clinical, temporary setting such as a hospital and impart the perception that they are long-term homes.

**Do Not Resuscitate (DNR) or No Code (NC):** An advanced directive that *is written* and *on the State Required Form* that expresses the individuals wishes not to undergo cardiopulmonary resuscitation (CPR) or advanced cardiac life support (ACLS) in the event they stop breathing or their heart stops beating. A DNR does not effect any treatment or efforts that would be appropriate to take prior to the heart stopping or the patient stops breathing. The common misconception is that someone who has a DNR will not receive antibiotics or other treatments.

**Fiduciary:** A legal or ethical relationship of trust between two or more parties. Typically, a fiduciary prudently takes care of money for another person who is either unwilling or unable to do so.

**Financial Power of Attorney (FPOA):** A limited form of POA that allows an individual to make financial decisions for another individual, usually when they become temporarily or permanently incapacitated.

**Guardianship:** A legal guardian is a person who has legal authority to act for an individual, usually due to disability or incapacitation. This status is awarded by a court.

**Guest:** In an effort to de-institutionalize the LTC industry, some companies refer to their patients as "Guests" implying a short or temporary stay.

**Healthcare Power of Attorney (HCPOA):** A limited form of POA that allows an individual to make healthcare decisions for another individual, usually when they become temporarily or permanently incapacitated.

**Home Health Agency (HH):** An agency that provides limited caregiving and medical assistance at a person's home. They may come in once a week to assist with a shower, they may come in and set up medisets, and they may even assist to the level of a full-time caregiver daily providing cooking, cleaning, laundry and caregiving assistance. HH Agencies may also provide in-home therapy and wound management.

**Hospice:** A type and philosophy of care that focuses on the palliation (comfort) of a terminally ill or seriously ill patient's pain and symptoms, and attending to their emotional and spiritual needs. Hospice is not necessarily just for terminal patients, but often is used to provide enhanced supportive care for seriously ill residents.

**Level of Care (LOC):** In some states, there are very formal definitions of various LOC's, while others do not specify. It is important to note that in states such as Arizona, AL's are licensed based upon LOC. For example Memory Care is considered Directed Care. Therefore a facility that is licensed for only Supervisory or Personal Care cannot accept or retain residents that are classified as Directed Care. The most common use of "LOC" is when it comes to the monthly bill and determining the frequency of Service Plans. More on LOC in chapters 10 and 11.

**Limited Power of Attorney:** A form of POA that can be any of the following; general, healthcare or financial. It may specify conditions in which the POA is active, and is generally only active for a limited amount of time. For example a limited POA may be executed when a family member is traveling, and they confer the authority outlined in the Limited POA for the month they are gone, after which it becomes void.

**Living Will:** An advance directive that is a set of written instructions or preferences that specify what actions should be taken if the individual is unable to make those decisions for themself. Usually a POA is responsible for following the guidelines in a Living Will. The Living Will may indicate the individual who is responsible for making these decisions, thus potentially negating the necessity for a HCPOA.

**Long Term Care (LTC) Facility:** A generalized term referring to a facility that serves the needs of individuals that require extended or permanent care by training care staff. Assisted Living, Memory Care, Skilled Nursing and Behavioral Health Facilities are all sometimes referred to as LTC facilities, however, LTC is also a specific term used by some insurance plans and facilities referring to a unit in their Skilled Nursing which houses residents permanently.

**LVN/LPN:** A licensed vocational nurse, or licensed practical nurse. States refer to the licensure differently, and the two are equivalent in training and certifications.

**Medicaid:** Government funded healthcare. Generally for lower income individuals. Medicaid is usually administered through a third party. Therefore, Medicaid may be referred to as "ALTCS", "AHCCCS" or the third party administering the benefits such as Mercy Care, Evercare and Bridgeway in Arizona.

**Mediset:** A daily medication organizer. You'll see these at drug stores with the days of the week on each separated compartment. The mediset can be set up once a week and medications consumed at the days/times indicated.

**Mental Health Power of Attorney (MHPOA or MPOA):** A limited form of POA that allows an individual to make healthcare decisions for another individual, usually when they become temporarily or permanently incapacitated specifically when cognition is involved. Many memory care and behavioral health facilities will not admit someone unless there is an MPOA.

**Nurse Practitioner (NP):** This is a nurse that has extensive training and often acts as a patient's primary care professional. They can write prescriptions, order tests and evaluate/diagnose disease.

**Physician (MD):** Medical Doctor.

**Physicians Assistant (PA):** Similar to a physician, the PA is often used as a primary care professional; however they require oversight from an MD.

**Power of Attorney (POA):** A written authorization by an attorney giving the authority for one individual to act in place of another. The holder of the POA does not hold any authority that supersedes the authority of the person granting the POA. For all POA types, the individual granting the POA (mom or dad) still retain their rights and they have the final say. A POA cannot override the wishes of the grantor. For that, a guardianship is usually needed. An exception may be for a Mental Health POA, and is only under very specific circumstances.

**Private Pay:** Refers to residents whose source of paying monthly fees comes from their own finances. This may include the residents income, family contributions or other assets.

**Resident:** In an effort to de-institutionalize the LTC industry, customers (those who live at these communities) are referred to as "Residents". Often they live there indefinitely, and it is considered less clinical than using the term "Patient".

**RN:** A registered nurse. RN's are often required at certain staffing levels in some types of facilities, notably in SNF's as well as in other facilities in a managerial role.

**Service Plan:** This is the list of identifiable conditions or considerations regarding the residents care developed at move-in, and during the duration of the resident's stay that outlines what preventative and maintenance actions the staff of the facility will take (chapter 14). These are required to be updated at specific intervals.

There are several types of care in Long Term Care: Independent Living (IL), Assisted Living (AL), Memory Care (MC), Skilled Nursing Facility (SNF) and Continuing Care Retirement Community (CCRC which is a combination of all).

**Independent Living**

Independent Living is not generally a regulated healthcare facility but I have included it for explanation. They are generally attached to, or part of, a larger CCRC (more on that later) or simply referred to as a "55+ community". The concept of the IL is to provide some services often found in an AL without the healthcare related care services and at a reduced cost. Examples of services offered at an IL are: laundry service, housekeeping, a dining room on site (with meals included in the base cost or at an additional fee), activities and transportation services.

The primary draw of an IL is convenience. A resident may be able to successfully complete their ADL's without assistance, but want the convenience of dining services, socialization, or they no longer want to keep up with household maintenance and cleaning. The transportation and dining service of an IL are often the most desirable features.

An IL does not provide assistance with ADL's therefore no service plan is created. If they do, they may run into licensing issues as the governing body may determine that they are in fact operating an unlicensed AL. They do not provide reminders or assistance with taking medications either as state licensing authorities require the individual themselves, a family member or nurse/caregiver to perform those tasks. However, some IL's work closely with Home Health agencies that can provide limited assistance with ADL's, including medication management.

An IL may also have very limited staff, and not have 24 hour staff. An IL can be thought of as an apartment complex with some concierge type services available.

### Assisted Living

The services at an AL include the services of an IL, with the added services of ADL assistance, medication administration assistance, and healthcare monitoring and maintenance. They have trained and certified 24 hour staff, they are required to meet certain resident safety requirements and often have a full-time nurse to supervise care.

The amount and frequency of services provided to their residents are outlined in the Service Plan. Resident health is monitored and tracked and the facility may assume every aspect of medication management (ordering, reordering, stocking and administration).

The Assisted Living concept has been developed to bridge the gap between individuals that can live comfortably and safely at home, and those that need constant, 24 hour medical care provided by a nurse or a physician.

**Memory Care (MC)** is a specialized form of Assisted Living. It generally has more structured routines, customized activity programs, specially trained staff and custom architectural considerations (such as access controlled entrances and exits) designed for individuals with dementia and alzheimers.

A **Behavioral Health** program can be a part of an AL, a SNF or a Group Home. The program is similar to a MC, however the residents primary diagnosis is usually not necessarily related to dementia or Alzheimer's. Traumatic Brain Injuries (TBI's), schizoeffective, bi-polar and other non-dementia/Alzheimer's disorders that result in behaviors are managed.

A **Group Home** is another form of AL with its own set of advantages and disadvantages when compared to a larger AL. Group Homes vary in size from 3-4 residents to around 10-15 depending on the specific states licensing requirements. They are generally run out of a converted residential house in a residential neighborhood. Generally the homes provide a more home like atmosphere, more personalized service and staff that know their residents extremely well because they are only taking care of 2 or 3 residents during their shift as opposed to meeting the needs of 15 or 20 during a typical shift at a larger assisted living. The disadvantages vary from potentially sacrificing the social aspect of a larger community, the quality of group homes are often hit or miss, and occasionally the services are not as all encompassing as a larger AL even though they can provide the vast majority of a residents needs. An example is that some homes are not equipped to handle residents with some forms of dementia.

## Skilled Nursing Facility

These are often referred to as a "Rehab Facility" or "Nursing Center". SNF's have RN's and LPN's on staff 24 hours a day, a staff physician that makes regular rounds and a dedicated rehabilitation team made up of occupational therapists, physical therapists and speech therapists.

Although some residents are living permanently in a SNF due to a condition that requires a nurse be available at all times, most individuals reside at a SNF short term. They may be recovering from an injury or illness, or they may have a chronic condition and their usual caregiver is unable to perform those tasks for a short period of time.

The intent of a SNF should be to recover the individual as quickly and safely as possible, then return them home. As mentioned before, long term care is also available at most SNF's for when a resident requires permanent care that supercedes that available at an AL.

Stays at a SNF are generally covered in whole or in part by Medicaid/Medicare and major medical insurance for specific intervals of time and may require co-pays by the resident. A SNF is the highest level of care short of a hospital and is extremely expensive. **Daily** rates vary from $150 a day, to well over $600 a day depending on the care and equipment required.

## Continuing Care Retirement Community

A CCRC is essentially a campus that includes several of the before mentioned types of facilities usually an IL, AL/MC and a SNF. The concept is that residents can age in place, fostering a healthier mind/body/spirit. If they start in IL, it is not necessary to move to another facility across town when they require AL services. Often, an IL or AL resident will continue to pay rent if they need short term rehab whereas in a CCRC there is occasionally a credit to the unoccupied apartment amongst other benefits. *If you are extremely short on time, and do not know what level of care your loved one needs, stop reading now and find CCRC's in the desired area.* The Case Managers, Social Workers and AL Nurses will be able to find the appropriate care setting for them.

Another advantage of a CCRC is that if they have an injury or illness, their friends or neighbors can simply walk down the hall to visit them while they recover in the SNF and they are near their friends in the IL/AL.

# Chapter 2

## When is it time to consider Long Term Care?

There are many reasons people consider LTC whether it be based upon need, convenience or piece of mind. In a healthy individual, all of their needs are being met sufficiently. When several of their needs are being overlooked or omitted, issues arise.

Needs are often summarized based upon **Maslow's hierarchy of needs**[1]. He identifies five basic categories: Physiological, Safety, Love/Belonging, Esteem and Self-actualization. These are the basic definitions, as defined by Maslow.

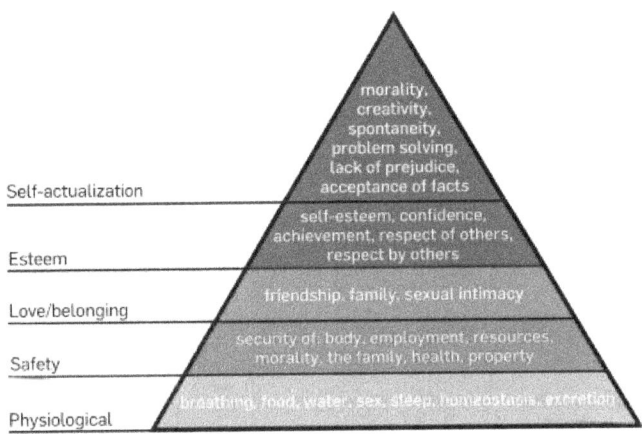

An interpretation of Maslow's hierarchy of needs, represented as a pyramid with the more basic needs at the bottom. en.wikipedia.org

**Physiological:** breathing, food, water, sex, sleep, homeostasis and excretion. In the healthcare world, often these are the needs which receive much of the focus.

**Safety:** security of body, employment, resources, morality, the family, health and property.

**Love/Belonging:** friendship, socialization, purpose, family and sexual intimacy.

**Esteem:** self-esteem, confidence, achievement, respect of others, respect by others.

**Self-actualization:** morality, creativity, spontaneity, problem solving, lack of prejudice, acceptance of facts.

The need for a LTC facility is realized when the individual begins to fail at meeting their basic needs. Perhaps one or many of these needs are being neglected. Most LTC facilities structure themselves to meet as many of these needs as possible for their residents in order to promote a healthy lifestyle. Each type of care facility can assist in meeting these needs to various degrees.

Throughout my career, I have helped families through just about every move-in scenario out there. I have simplified those into two categories; "Routine/Planned" and "Emergency".

The **"Routine/Planned"** family have perhaps noticed over a period of time that mom or dad need a little more help with their everyday lives. They usually live alone, and the adult children have found that more and more frequently they are called upon to help with things that perhaps they never had to before. This can range from collecting mail to paying bills, maybe doing laundry once a week or driving them to appointments. They may have noticed some weight loss because their loved one has stopped making regular trips to the grocery store or are not eating properly. On some occasions they notice that prescription bottles are empty and have not been refilled either because their parent cannot make it to the pharmacy or they've simply forgotten to do so.

The children are often put in the position of deciding whether to move their parents into their own house. Quite often there is not sufficient room in the house, or they would be left alone the majority of the day when their children go to work. In some cases, parents do not want to burden their children and refuse any attempt at help.

These families will generally contact the community and say that they are looking for a place for their parents because they need more help than they can provide themselves, or they have started to become reclusive, or there are health complications due to lack of exercise and/or proper nutrition. Often the children live out of state or a great distance away that precludes them from being of regular help.

There is usually some time to slowly introduce their parent to the idea of an LTC facility of some sort, and show them how living at an LTC community will be of benefit. This process can take anywhere from several weeks to years.


**"Emergency"** move-ins are just that. The family has been caught unaware of a condition, there has been some sort of life changing injury or manifestation of cognitive difficulties and occasionally even abuse or exploitation by someone they depend on.

Often very little information can be gathered during an emergency move-in and as a result, the community may be put in a position to accept liability if the resident is injured or suffers a health complication due to the staff being unaware of an issue. Falls, medication mismanagement and injury to themselves and others are often results of even well managed emergency move-ins. As a result, some communities will not entertain the idea of an emergency move-in and often will require a certain waiting period while medical and assessment information is reviewed to ensure they can meet that residents needs.

One such case of an emergency move-in is illustrated below.

### "Linda"

Linda had two sons, both of whom lived out of state. She had lived in the same house for over 40 years and alone for the last 20 after her husband passed away. Her neighborhood was once very desirable, but in the last few decades had declined. The area was now known for drug dealers and had a significant homeless presence along the canal system that bordered the neighborhood on the west side.

One evening, she had decided to go to the grocery store...at 3am, which is obviously a very risky activity in her neighborhood. She was noticed by a passerby and a city police officer made contact with her as she wandered along a major road 2 miles from her house. She had no ID, no purse and she was rambling incoherently about going to the grocery store. Unable to get her name he drove her around the neighborhood for the better part of an hour until she managed to identify her house which allowed the officer to identify her through the department of transportation database. He took her to the local emergency room where she was transported to an acute psych hospital. The staff at the facility where unable to contact the sons until day 6. They jumped on planes and arrived the next day.

I first met the sons when they arrived at my community as we were the closest one to their mother's house and they had seen the building before when visiting. The sons were completely overwhelmed by the situation. Our community happened to have skilled nursing, assisted living and memory care. After speaking with the social worker in our skilled nursing, he was referred to AL. Not only did they have no clue their mother had any cognitive issue, they had very little guidance from the social worker at the psych hospital. They were simply told to find a "nursing home" for their mother as she was not cognitively able to care for herself.

I spent several hours with the sons to get some background information on their mother and we agreed to meet at the psych hospital the next afternoon. When I met Linda, she seemed initially to be in control of her faculties. After another 5 minutes of attempted conversation it was obvious she was confused and her words began to become jumbled, a condition coined in the industry as "word salad". She obviously could not live alone as she would be unable to communicate with the general public, her bank, the grocery store staff and would not be able to communicate her needs in an emergency. In fact, as her 3am wandering proved, she could not even identify when she was in danger.

The staff said she had a mild urinary tract infection and it could account for some of the confusion. They also noted that she had not bathed in quite some time. She was constantly attempting to leave the hospital, without any identification or even shoes!

Following her interview, the charge nurse said that she would be discharged in two days. No wonder the sons were so overwhelmed! This is unfortunately a common situation in healthcare. The hospital will sometimes only give 48 hours notice before discharge. This puts a lot of pressure on families, making an otherwise stressful situation even more so. In this case, the short notice was compounded by the inability to contact the family for quite some period of time. Even hospitals are misinformed when it comes to AL vs SNF's these days. Whereas a SNF has a pharmacy on call and stocks their own medications and supplies, an AL has to order these specifically. Sometimes, depending upon the insurance, items are not obtainable by the AL and family are responsible for acquiring those items.

Needless to say, the sons were extremely lucky to have walked through our doors that day. With very little help from the psych hospital, they just happened to walk into a community that could meet their mother's needs and had a vacancy. They easily could have burned through that 48 hour notice trying to find a suitable community.

In this case, the community nurse and I determined that Linda was appropriate for our memory care in assisted living. She moved in at the end of the day after the 48 hour notice expired. There was very little time for her sons to do any kind of research. They did not have powers of attorney prepared, nor any other advanced directives. The community nurse accompanied one of the brothers to Linda's house and found a stock of medications that had been automatically delivered to her via her pharmacy. This also provided information on Linda's Primary Care Physician which we were able to contact and confirm her current medication list. The doctors office also informed us of several other medical conditions that existed and which were easily addressed in her Service Plan.

The key to an emergency move-in is full cooperation with the care center staff and the family in order to ensure a safe environment for the resident. Both the staff and family should expect to do a lot of leg work and constantly communicate with the other to keep them informed of progress. I cannot tell you how many times a family has simply shown up at an AL and the staff had no idea they were coming because the family assumed everything was taken care of when in actuality there was a miscommunication and something important was missed.

# Chapter 3

## Prepping your parents for the move

This is a very tricky subject and the strategy employed to gain your parents acceptance varies greatly. There is a long lasting stigma associated with "nursing homes" amongst our older generations that a "home" is the place you go to wither away and die. Our elders have seen their neighbors, friends and family be sequestered to a home and they stop calling, sending holiday cards and then eventually they receive the news they have passed. While there is truth in this, it is far from the absolute truth.

The truth is that most people do not move to a LTC if they are perfectly healthy. There is a medical or cognitive issue that necessitates their move. Unfortunately these conditions are usually progressive and the outcome is inevitable. What most seniors do not see is that while at such a community the residents are engaged in daily social activities and they are able to pursue their previous hobbies and interests with assistance. It is not that they are "withering away", in fact they are thriving and living a higher quality of life than their neighbor who spends hours sitting at the front window watching the traffic drive by hoping for visitors.

When it comes to prepping for the move in an emergency move-in, there is very little time for prepping. The nature of emergency move-ins will require that all of those involved are open, honest and come to grips with the situation and the potential changes in a short amount of time. All of the other routine or planned move-ins may allow long term discussions and the potential resident will have time to contemplate and understand the change. It is usually not a successful plan of action to show up at mom's house and say "We don't think you are doing very well here, we are moving you to a home." You can expect your loved one to instantly dig their heels in as they associate a very morbid existence to that comment. It is akin to saying "We think you are not going to be around much longer, so let's go pick out a coffin."

The approach taken depends solely on your relationship with the potential resident as well as their own perception of their needs. If you know of a friend of theirs that currently lives in an LTC Community, start by taking them to visit for lunch or to participate in a community event. Most communities have a wide range of monthly activities from outings to the theater, museums, art galleries as well as guest speakers on topics ranging from financial preparedness to presentations on subjects they might find interesting. In one community I've managed, we had an archaeologist bring in artifacts from the Sonoran desert and spent nearly two hours talking about early life in the desert. It was a very popular presentation. In another community, a retired Secretary of State brought a copy of his memoirs and reminisced with the other residents about the changes that have impacted all of their lives over the last 50 years.

Once your loved one begins to see the diverse list of activities and people, they often begin to change their perspective. Don't forget about the food! Stay for lunch or dinner. The marketing representative for the community will usually be more than happy to provide a free meal to prospective residents and their families. Since most large communities operate their meals based upon an open menu and a restaurant style model, the dining experience is a strong draw. Every meal is like going out to eat.

The staff interactions can be another good resource. Engage the staff in conversation and ask them question about how they like working there, what their job is, and why they chose to do their job. The staff should be a strong ally in your attempts to win your prospective resident over. They are often significantly compensated for making an impact on a residents move-in decision, so ensure your tell the administration if someone makes a difference. Another aspect is that you are interviewing the staff. Not all communities are staffed by the same people. Since these are the people that will be serving your loved one for quite a while, they should be compatible and easily create repoire.

Some prospective residents cannot be won over by the community itself. They are not particularly social and prefer to spend time reading, etc. Although most communities have significant sharing libraries, it is a source of anxiety to be around so many people all the time. As I said earlier, you need to determine what works for your particular loved one. An honest, rational discussion of their needs may be the best approach, and the one that I prefer that families have before a move. Part of this discussion should include preparing or updating Powers of Attorney (general, financial, mental, healthcare), advance directives (living will, do not resuscitate) and obtaining financial information (names of banks, account numbers, investments, properties, etc).

It may seem easier, especially if you are very uncomfortable, to put the brunt of the preparation on the community staff. This is not wise. While the community and staff can represent their advantages and paint everything in a rosy color, when issues arise (and they will even in the best teams) it compounds any misgivings the resident had when they moved in. The worst scenarios involving move-ins are when the adult children have misled their parents regarding the nature of their move. The following is a specific example.

**"John and Mary"**

John and Mary were married octogenarians that had been together for over 60 years. They had three children, all of which lived locally. They both had very mild cognitive issues that resulted in forgetfulness and they had stopped bathing regularly. Their medications were always running out and the children would constantly find pills on the floor when they came over to clean. The children decided it was time to move their parents to Assisted Living.

John and Mary had lived in a rural ranch home for their entire lives. The isolation and lack of neighbors coupled with financial considerations (their ranch was now worth millions and their bank accounts and retirement savings had dwindled to nearly nothing) put the children in a bad situation as they would be hard pressed to continue to support their parents financially and although they were already rotating through taking turns cleaning, bathing and grocery shopping for their parents, their own family needs were being neglected.

Initially, John and Mary accepted their move into an AL. They thought it would be a nice place to stay for a time and even helped pick out what they wanted to move with them. Things were going very well, they were very social and well liked amongst the other residents and staff and their lifetime of ranching had a very visible effect on their physical fitness. A month into their stay, the nurse and caregivers began to report that John and Mary were asking with more and more frequency when they could move back home. The nurse was concerned their cognition was declining, and sat down with them to explain their current situation. When the nurse explained that this *was* their home, she was completely caught off guard by their reactions. Mary broke down into tears and John became verbally abusive. That night they packed their bags and spent the following three days in a constant attempt to leave.

I met with John and Mary to help determine how we were going to keep them safe and comfortable, and to find out what had changed so suddenly. Through the course of the conversation, I discovered that their children had told them that their ranch house had a termite infestation and that they needed to stay with us while they had the house treated and repaired. They did not tell them that they were moving permanently. I called their children, and was informed that their ranch had sold the day before. They asked me to pass this information on to their parents. I refused, and the next day the children visited and explained everything to their parents.

Mary began to slip into an ever deeper depression, and John stopped doing his daily exercise routines. Within three months Mary was transferred to our memory care and John passed away 6 months after that.

While their intentions were good, by not being honest with their parents because it was too uncomfortable for them to do so, the adult children put their parents in a bad situation that affected their emotional well being. Creating a pleasant, nonstressful move is as important, or in some cases, more important than the care that residents will receive once they arrive. In this case, I believe that John and Mary felt that their family had turned their back on them, treated them without respect, and moved them into the AL to let nature take its course. **They lost control of their lives at that moment, which took the purpose from their lives and ultimately their drive to live for the next day.** These unintentional consequences, and John and Mary's belief in such, actually brought that to fruition.

Do not mislead someone into moving into a community. People have rights and deserve respect, they are fully grown human beings and forcing someone into a LTC is paramount to sentencing them to prison of sorts. Keep in mind that most people in their 80's and 90's have lived through the Great Depression, World War II, the Cold War and the social unrest of the 60's and 70's. They are usually very independent, strong willed people that view the move to a structured LTC facility as a loss of their independence and in some cases a loss of identity. These issues have to be addressed and presented to them in a way that they understand and accept this new stage in their life.

## Documents to prepare

Talk about and prepare:

Living Will

Do Not Resuscitate (if desired)

Powers of Attorney

Medical, Financial, Mental, Healthcare

Bank Account Information

Long Term Care Insurance information

Copies of ID Cards

Drivers license, insurance cards

Pet information

Vet information, vaccinations, licensing

## Accept some changes

I mention this because a facility will require the resident to accept a level of openness and participation. You do not want the label of "noncompliant". It will throw up roadblocks to admission for all but the facilities most desperate for new admissions and that label will stay in the medical record permanently. The resident must be forthcoming with changes to the way they feel, and share any physician orders/instructions with staff. The resident must be a willing participant in care plans and understand that if they choose not to participate, they could be asked to move elsewhere. Also, there may be a good reason to change physicians or specialists, usually based on location and availability of transportation.

Examples of this are those who drink too much or abuse prescription medications. These both create liability on behalf of the facility and in almost every case the resident will be given notice to vacate after the staff attempt interventions. **DO NOT RELY ON THE STAFF** of a facility to detox. They are not substance abuse professionals. If substance abuse is an issue, seek professional help prior to the move.

# Chapter 4

## Affording Long Term Care

The cost of living in an LTC community can be extreme as previously mentioned. Although many retirees have accounted for the increase in cost of living, many have not. Many more lost a significant amount of money in the stock market a few years ago. At one community I saw a 10% decrease in residents as their investments tanked and their 10 years of AL finances quickly dwindled to several months. These residents were forced to move in with family, acquire state assistance, or in some cases the stress had severe detrimental effects on their health.

So, how much money will they actually need? This is not a cut and dry question. Generally monthly costs of LTC are based on the frequency and intensity of care. There may also be a "buy in" required that could cost 10's of thousands of dollars...before they even move in. Some quick phone calls to local LTC's should give you a general range of costs for each. Be warned, some community sales staff will not provide cost over the phone. They want the opportunity to showcase their community and demonstrate why it is worth the premium price.

The average annual cost of LTC ranges from $30,000/year ($2,500/month) to well over $90,000/year ($7,500/month. The type of care and monthly cost are closely related and dependent upon location. The average length of stay in an AL is roughly 2 ½ years. If you assume $3500/month as an average monthly stay (which is about right in my area), then the resident will spend approximately $100,000 over that 2.5 years. This does not include continence supplies, medications and other ancillary costs. You will be able to calculate actual costs once you talk to the community and the resident is assessed at a level of care. The purpose and how to assist in an accurate assessment is covered in chapter 11.

There are many ways to come up with the cost associated with LTC. Insurance is a big help, but very limited. Usually a significant portion of Skilled Nursing is covered by Medicare and supplemental insurance for an extended period of time, usually around 100 days. That's roughly 3 ½ months. Enough time to recover from an illness or injury, but if a long-term or permanent injury is sustained limiting the individuals ability to care for themselves safely, the referral is usually made to an AL or skilled LTC.

Some seniors have purchased specific **LTC Insurance Policies** or have LTC riders (addendums) attached to their Medicare supplement insurance. This is very different from Medicare or any standard Medicare supplements. LTC policies generally pay a set rate per day to the policy holder for every day they are in an LTC setting that meets the requirements put forth in their policy. Find the policy and contact the agent for a good explanation of the requirements to receive payments. Also, the community will not be responsible for filing claims. Claims are filed by the policy holder or POA and payments are received directly to the resident or the POA. Until those payments are received (usually there is an exclusion period that ranges from 2 weeks to 90 days), the resident is still responsible to pay the community all necessary fees.

As many of our seniors have military service, they may qualify for **VA Benefits**. The qualifications are based upon several factors, and as with anything government related, are complicated. If a potential resident or spouse of a resident had any military service, contact a VA representative and start the process for approval as soon as you start considering AL or IL, as it generally takes 6 months for the veteran to get approval (and often up to a year for a spouse). The nice thing is that the VA benefits are retroactive, so even if you are faced with an emergency move-in, the VA will still pay for time in a facility while your application was being processed. If you contact the VA and are still completely confused, there are private VA consultants that can help prepare the application, and usually they are also financial planners that may be able to help with other aspects of your prospective resident's finances.

**Medicaid** is a viable option for individuals without significant assets. It generally covers the AL costs (not including ancillary charges) that are directly related to healthcare. The program is usually run by the county and qualification requires application and ongoing review by a case manager. In Arizona, the county contracts out servicing Medicaid to private companies to administer benefits. The Resident will have a "share of cost" which means that the majority of their monthly income will go to the community and they will be allowed to keep a small percentage for personal use, around a $100 per month. Many communities do not accept Medicaid as it generally pays the community well below their private pay rates and they do not want the hassle of going through the billing process every month.

Other **assets** that should be considered are properties owned, vehicles and personal belongings. The sale of a house is usually the first step taken to liquidate assets as the home will not be used by the resident. Sale of a house can be time consuming, and the facility should be made aware if the residents stay will be dependent upon the sale of the house. The facility Director may be willing to provide some leeway in making payments if they know you are waiting on a house to sell. Savings, investment accounts and pension plans are generally the last line of money available. Meet with a financial advisor and work out a plan based upon what your loved one can afford. That will help narrow down the facilities to those that are affordable.

In addition to assets, a person will have ADL requirements that must be met to qualify for Medicaid programs and some diagnosis will help meet the criteria (such as dementia or Alzheimers).

Some Medicaid programs use a point system. This means the member must meet a certain "score" on their ADL's to qualify for Medicaid assistance with monthly rent at a community. An assessment by the community or another healthcare professional can assist in determining if the ADL needs meet the point cutoff for assistance. Keep in mind that a person does not necessarily require "hands on" assistance with ADL's to count those points. The person may require verbal reminders, cueing or standby assist. All of those are helpful in gaining the necessary points to qualify.

# Chapter 5

## Determining needs

The best way to determine exactly what kind of senior care the resident needs is to get to know them and their daily routines. This is similar to what a nurse or AL manager will do when they perform their assessment. Reach out to their physician, family and their friends as a source of information. Physical and medical needs are the first things to consider and in a rushed move-in, perhaps all that can be determined. Help with ADL's, medication management and memory care are three of the big ones. Once you know what level of care they will need, you can eliminate quite a few facilities and homes.

Do some investigating if there is time and find exactly what you are looking for in a community. If your parents are active in an adult activity group or club, make sure the communities you are looking at can provide transportation to the group, or even a space for the groups to meet.

Create a "hard list" and a "soft list" of needs and wants. This is very similar to looking for a house and the surrounding neighborhood. Instead of looking at closet space, local schools, proximity to the grocery store, you are looking at activity programs, on-site beauty shops, exercise room, etc. A community can have a wonderful activity program, but if your loved one is not interested in social activities...and never has, it is unlikely they'll suddenly become more social. Do they like constant activity around them? If so a larger CCRC type of community may be desirable, if they like things quieter, then a group home may be preferable. Ask the community marketing representative to eat lunch at the community…don't make an appointment ahead of time, show up and ask for the marketing director and let them know you'd like to see the dining room and try the food. If it is possible to bring your prospective resident, do it. After all, they'll be the ones eating the food, not you. This is also a great opportunity to see the population of the AL. Do they look happy? Is there conversation going on at their tables while they eat? Are the residents willing to engage you in conversation? What do they think about the food, activities and care? Are the dining staff friendly and attentive? Does the food look like it was prepared well and placed on the plate to look appetizing?

Specialized programming. If memory care is a necessity, make sure you find a community that has as specialized a memory care as possible. Too many AL's were built as AL's, and the memory care is an afterthought. In fact, specialized training for MC staff is often nonexistent or inadequate.

Location. Do you want to visit? Do you want them to be close to their friends so their friends can visit? Another thing to consider is staff. If you choose an AL way out in the middle of nowhere, the community will have certain challenges, one of which is adequate staff and maybe staff retention.

What levels of care do the communities provide?

Independent Living may be a good option for a resident who needs meals prepared, housekeeping or laundry, transportation, socialization and someone available to summon help. They are not for residents who require regular assistance with ADL's, medication administration or health monitoring. For that, an Assisted Living should be considered. An AL will have staff dedicated to assisting residents with ADL's. An AL may have dedicated personnel to administer medications. They will note any changes in their residents and notify physicians. The drawback to Assisted Living is that often there is not a nurse on staff 24 hours a day. Well trained caregivers can and do handle nearly anything that can happen in an AL, but if there is a treatment or medication that requires a nurse on hand at any time of the day, then a Skilled Nursing Facility may be required. A SNF also usually staffs their CNA's at a much higher ratio than an AL does caregivers because residents in a SNF usually require much more frequent care.

# Chapter 6
## Researching Communities

Once you know what you are looking for, the next challenge is finding it. A simple internet search will generally bring up many, many options. Review the webpages closely for levels of care offered, amenities offered and some will even have their activities calendar posted. Once you find a few options, research those specific communities. Again an internet search will provide you with several websites which review them based on others' experiences. Another resource is your state regulatory website which will have the facilities license status as well as the managers' license status. Personal referrals are also very valuable as well as professional referrals.

Most of the resources listed below are web based. The reasoning for this is that if you are in a time crunch, you do not want to waste the little time you do have on the phone, listening to sales pitches or physically visiting each facility. By using a smart web based approach, you can focus your efforts on facilities that meet your needs.

## Web searches

One of the easiest ways to find some likely candidates is to plug "Assisted Living in [insert your city or zip code]" or "Group Homes in [location]". The big three providers such as Brookdale, Sunrise and Emeritus will likely pop up first followed by some regional competitors. Group Homes may be less likely to have developed websites which may necessitate the need to find a local placement agent.

Follow the links to their websites and scroll through to see what the community offers. Keep your checklist list handy and start checking the boxes. This is not a final list however, as often community websites are not fully up to date, and it is unlikely you will find too much pricing information.

Once you've found a few communities that seem to matchup to the majority of your needs, search them by name on the internet. There will be several websites dedicated to reviewing facilities that will come up, usually after the company links do. Several sites allow users to rank the communities and leave comments. Be aware that often the comments are left by disgruntled ex-residents, or even on occasion ex-employees. The ratings may deviate significantly based upon how recent the ratings were done, and how popular the website is. Don't make your decision based solely off of those comments unless they have so many poor reviews and they seem to have a common theme throughout, such as poor staffing, poor maintenance, high staff turnover, etc. Read through the provider mission statement or care philosophy on their website. There are some companies that while they tout their "resident first" concept, in reality you will find many reviews or even company distributed statements that state "bottom line first, employees are second and resident care and welfare are third". To be fair, these companies are in the business of making a profit. You want to find the companies that pay more than lip service to the concept of balancing the bottom line with resident care. Also temper this information with the knowledge that the vast majority of people that work at the actual community taking care of residents are not making huge incomes…they do it because they love what they do.

## Agency and State Regulatory Websites

Most states now have online databases of licensed facilities. You can simply go to the state Department of Health website and find the long term care section. You can generally search by name, address or license number. This is a very powerful tool to determine how good the facility is at taking care of their residents. Most communities undergo annual surveys where a state inspector will visit, review their records and create a report indicating what the facilities shortcomings are. Again, take this with somewhat of a grain of salt, because you will only find negative information in the report. Any violation of department guidelines is usually cited. Read each citation carefully, as usually if the facility is cited it is cited for more than one occurrence.

The violations to look for are medication related, service plan related and life safety violations (non-functional fire control system, no fire drills, unsecured doors, inoperable air conditioners or heaters) which may indicate that the facility is not keeping up with basic concerns.

## Examples of warning signs:

**Medications:** The way medications are tracked are via a sheet of paper called a "MAR" or Medication Administration Record. Every time a medication is given to a resident, it is recorded on the MAR. Occasionally the nurse or medication technician administering the medication either incorrectly completes the form, or omits important information. Each time that happens, DHS is likely to issue a line item citation. If you review a facilities survey results and you find multiple, multiple medication errors such as "Medications not available"

41

, "Physician orders not followed" , "Wrong medication given to the wrong resident"…then there may be some supervision, training or other issues in that building.

**Care:** If a community has multiple citations with issues such as hydration, odors, resident cleanliness, diet orders, etc…then there may also be issues at the community especially if this is repeated survey after survey.

Quite often, serious medication and care issues are cited hand-in-hand.

**Clerical/Documentation:** The amount of information that facilities are required to track is astounding. The facility may be cited for clerical or documentation issues ranging from a service plan not signed by the resident or responsible party, to a weight missing from a service plan. These are relatively minor infractions, but if you see long lists of residents who had these things missing, then this may indicate several things. The facility may be short staffed, the staff may be undertrained, or it could mean absolutely nothing, people make mistakes.

*No community gets out of a survey with zero deficiencies. 10 or less citations of minor issues can be considered an "A".* If you review their surveys and you find citations for things such as employee files being incomplete or water temperature is too high, likely the surveyor did not find anything critical during their survey. That is a good thing.

The manager of the community, sometimes referred to as the Administrator, Director or Executive Director will also have a license. If you know the managers' name, you can search their history as well for any administrative or disciplinary action taken against them by the state. A good director will never have had their license suspended or revoked. Any strikes on their license should be carefully and critically scrutinized.

If you know the managers name, you can try searching for them on Linkedin, a professional networking website which usually has a summary of their work experience. How long have they been in the industry? How many companies have they worked for in the last year? Has their career been successful, or have they bounced back and forth between being a manager and being a caregiver or salesperson? Some managers are specialists and are employed by companies for a short period of time as a "fixer". Ask the manager that does not stay at a place for more than a few months at a time.

All of these may factor into your decision as someone with a long history of being a caregiver and then becoming a manager may be more focused on resident care, whereas someone who has been in marketing that becomes a manager may be more focused on revenue and have less knowledge of how a long term care facility works at the care level. In my opinion, the best managers are those that have worked in multiple aspects of a care facility.

## Referral Agencies and Placement Agents

There is an entire industry that is based around independent consultants that assist in the placement of seniors into long term care facilities. These agents are analogous to a real estate agent. They generally do not charge their client, but the facility pays them upon move-in, usually a portion of the amount of first months' rent.

Some placement agents can move in 3 or more people per month. That is a significant income which buys you a significant time commitment by that agent and they do the majority of the leg work for you in order to earn that paycheck. They generally know the community and the facilities within it very well. They know about group homes and which communities will meet your needs and those that should be avoided.

There is a significant caveat to using a placement agent. Some of them will only show you communities that have agreed to pay their rates. If a facility does not pay placement agents, then they will not waste their time by showing them to you as they would not get paid. **This is not true of *all* placement agents and referral agencies but it is common. Ask your agent if they work this way.** Some religious based or non-profit agencies will not avoid the non-paying facilities, but you very well may never know. In my experience, most companies will prefer to hire and train a professional marketing team than rely on spending 3 or 4x's their salaries on outside referral agents. It is best to use an agency to augment your search, rather than rely on them solely.

### Other resources

There are also industry specific resources that may be useful. In Arizona the Assisted Living Federation of America (ALFA) and the Arizona Healthcare Association (AHCA) are both good resources. They provide links to those resources already described that can help with placement, referrals to assist with financing and also information on the facilities themselves.

**Personal referrals.** This may be one of the more important sources. If you know someone that has direct experience with the facility in question, they will likely give you the most honest answer of how the place actually works…the good and the bad. If they are current residents, family members of residents or staff, they should have an opinion. Again, do not neglect to contact friends and families for their recommendations.

# Chapter 7
## Making Contact

There are several ways to make contact with the communities you've spent so much time researching.

You can hire a placement agent. These agents will have an idea what communities have the items on your "hard" list, but keep in mind they may exclude or talk down some of the communities that are not willing to pay them for the referral.

You can set up an appointment by emailing or calling the community. Be aware that while a phone call will give you the ability to answer many of your questions quickly, you will also be put on "the list". I am referring to the salespersons lead database. Once you call, your name, phone number and other contact information is entered into the database and the salesperson is prompted to make contact with you at regular intervals by their marketing software on their computer. This can be useful to you, but may also be quite annoying when your phone is constantly ringing from sales calls. Make it a point to tell the salesperson how you prefer them to contact you. This will limit your personal stress and limit the annoying calls. If you email the community, often the salesperson will attempt to redirect you to a phone call and may not give much hard information until you do so. Even then, well trained salespeople will not give specific pricing and other community information until they meet with you face to face. This is usually a good idea. Often it is not possible to directly compare prices for communities based upon a price list. This is due to different amenities, staffing levels and included services. It is best to meet and review everything in detail.

You can walk in unannounced. This is my favorite. You have the opportunity to experience initial impressions of the staff, the building and the residents when they don't know you are coming and are not prepared. You can keep your contact information private, although usually there is an information card you will be asked to fill out while you wait which generally has a box to check indicating your contact preferences. You will still go into the database, but you will not receive the multitude of phone calls and emails. If there is no box on that card or sheet of paper indicating your contact preferences, write it across the top of the paper.

If you decide to walk in unannounced, you may want to be prepared for a wait. Most LTC's do not have a huge sales staff and those staff are usually pretty busy. If another tour is in the building, you may have to wait. Take advantage of this time…while waiting in the lobby you will get to observe the community which provides another great opportunity to gather information. "Is there dust in the corners?" How well kept is the building? Is it clean? Is the furniture outdated? What do the residents look like and act like? If their clothes are clean, their hair done well and they are smiling, it gives the community a boost in credibility. If the staff are not well dressed, or seem rushed and avoid eye contact, then perhaps they are relying on few too staff or the staff are not treated well.

When you walk in unannounced, you can expect to receive your "tour". The facility representative will walk you around, ask you a few questions, and try to sell you on their community so be prepared to spend anywhere from a half hour to an hour if your initial impressions keep that facility in the running.

# Chapter 8

## "The Tour"

This is your opportunity to "meet" the community. It can take anywhere from a half hour to several hours. This is the best time to get your questions answered and to actually see what the community has to offer.

Ideally, you need to bring the person that will be living there for the tour. Have your list of needs and wants ready. A good marketer will want to identify what your needs are so they can determine first of all if the community is an appropriate fit, and second to showcase how the community can meet your needs. Most communities will have an "Inquiry" form for you to fill out that has similar information on it. If you fill out the Appendix A form, make multiple copies and hand it to the community marketing representative, they should be able to determine quickly whether their community will be a fit for your loved one. It will also save you time because you do not have to sit in their lobby and fill out their form. Instead you can start working on your visit checksheet.

If your mother or father hates bingo, there is no point wasting everyone's time by sitting in on a bingo game in progress. If the marketing representative, or other staff member that is there to give you a tour just sets off and points at things, go ahead and end the tour and ask for someone else to contact you. That person likely will be wasting your time and are likely filling in for someone else. You want to respect your time and spend it determining if the community meets your residents defined needs and to answer your questions.

A good sales person will start the tour or sales interview by asking you questions. Most common questions you can expect to be asked are:

*For whom are you looking for a place to live?*

They want to gather the prospect's name as well as your relationship to them to determine if you are the decision maker or whether you are a placement agent or simply shopping around.

*What needs does your loved one need met?*

This question is to determine how critical the need is. Often this is where the story about mom wandering the streets at 3am comes out. This is also where a good salesperson will start putting together their version of your "hard list". They should then tailor the rest of the tour to showcase how their community meets your needs. If they do not answer how their community can meet your needs, then ask them at the end to address each of those needs.

*When do you anticipate a move?*

If you have just started looking and don't plan to move for 6 months, the salesperson will make a note of that. If you answered the previous question with "mom is in the hospital and the case worker says she shouldn't return home", then they will treat you much differently and probably show you specific apartments that are available and even give you some documents that would need to be filled out prior to the move, etc.

## What questions to ask

If you are asked to wait, ask to see their most recent survey if you were unable to locate it online. In Arizona having a copy of the survey available is a state requirement. If they do not have one, then they are not starting off well. When you meet with the salesperson, ask them about the deficiencies listed on the survey and how they've been fixed. The salesperson may not know, but they should find the right person that can. Remember this to see if someone ever does follow up with you. That is a great indicator of how engaged the management is which is directly related to the quality of care.

Do not expect to be able to ask all of these questions during the visit, but below are a few key questions that are often asked to get you started.

Ask to meet the Manager/Executive Director. Do not be surprised if the Manager is not available. They are generally very busy meeting with families, vendors, or preparing reports for their higher ups. If you do meet with the Manager, a few things to ask them may be:

*How long have you worked here?*

*Why did you decide to work for this company?*

*What is your vision for the community?*

…and my favorite:

*What challenges does the community have?*

The Manager will likely be very well polished in their answers and give you a company line. I like that last question, because it was often asked to me. If the Manager seems honest and open, then they likely will be that way when you move in. If they actually give you some "real" challenges, then to me that is very important that they have enough confidence in their staff to overcome those challenges. In fact, ask them *HOW* they are addressing those challenges.

Talk to the nurse if the community has one. Nurses are generally extremely busy, and they may not have time to meet with you. After all, nurses are very resident oriented and you are not their priority. Their residents are and they should put their care needs ahead of meeting with family of prospective residents. That is actually a good thing.

Ask the same questions you asked the Manager as the nurse is usually in charge when the Manager is out or unavailable. Be aware of generic "feel good" canned responses. If they give them to you, then likely you will get the same line when an issue arises.

Other nursing questions may be:

*What are your responsibilities in the facility?*

*What days or hours do you work?*

*What if my resident needs a nurse when you are not in the building?*

*How do we order medications?*

*Is there a physician on call?*


Other questions you may want to ask the Manager or nurse:

*How many residents do each caregiver take care of? (known as the staffing ratio…)*

*How many medication technicians do you have working at a time?*

*What kind of training do the caregivers receive?*

*Is there a visiting physician/dentist/optician/hearing aid service?*

*Transportation. Will you call 911 each and every    time something comes up, or do they provide    transportation for more routine medical issues? What are    their    transportation hours and cost?*

*Are there restrictions on visiting hours?*

Talk to staff as they pass by in the hall. Also pay attention to how professionally they are dressed, whether they acknowledge you with a smile or if they seem stressed out or too busy to talk. All of these can be indicators of their training, professionalism and whether your loved one will be comfortable with them. Can you understand them or do they have thick accents? If you are introduced to the staff, ask them:

*How long have you worked here?*

*Why do you like working for [company]?*

*Why did you decide to become a caregiver?*

Talk to residents. Don't grill everyone on the community, but try to gauge how happy they are to be working and living there.

*How do you like living here?*

*How is the food?*

*Why did you decide to choose this place?*

Pay attention to the cleanliness and state of repair of the building. If you see damaged walls or damaged fixtures, very dusty fixtures, etc. Ask how long it has been that way. If they say it is being repaired that day, then remember to check on it if you revisit the facility. If it hasn't been touched, then you may want to consider how honest the community staff are.

Look at the activity calendar, which should be posted, and see if what is listed is actually happening. Ask them how they conduct the activities, and whether your loved ones favorite activity/hobby can be added if it is not already on the schedule.

*A good tip is to take notes on the community literature that they gave you at the beginning of the tour or the checklist you started while initially beginning your search. Some companies will not hand out pamphlets or brochures to you until the end of the tour. Explain to them that you like to take notes and for organization's sake you make your notes on the community brochure and they will probably be more than happy to provide you one at the beginning. This way you will not lose the information for specific communities or it will not get mixed up with another community.*

## Chapter 8B: Regional Considerations

If the facility is located in a zone that has a high likelihood of a natural disaster, it may be a good idea to review their disaster or evacuation plan with the Manager. During Hurricane Katrina, I was working for the State of Texas and helped in the disaster relief. I was greatly disappointed with the way residents were dealt with before, during and after the hurricane hit New Orleans. In some cases the staff simply abandoned them, and in other situations they were without food and water for extended periods of time other than what the staff could scrounge up. Several years later, I helped prepare a community that was outside of the storm zone to receive residents from a sister community prior to another storm's arrival. The community maintained stocks of canned food and bottled water in case there was a disruption in their supply chain.

A facility in a very hot or cold environment may have a backup generator to run air conditioning/heating or critical medical equipment (such as oxygen concentrators) in the event that they lose power.

In Arizona, it is common to have a plan to move a resident temporarily to another room if their air conditioning stops working until it is repaired. Usually they stay in a guest suite or even the model apartment. Ask how long after the A/C stops working before they start considering moving the resident. I've seen some poorly managed communities allow a resident or multiple residents to live in an apartment for several days or even weeks before they receive approval/funds to repair their A/C. It is not unheard of for apartments to exceed 100°F during an Arizona summer without A/C which poses a significant risk to an elderly individual.

# Chapter 9

## After the Tour

After you've seen the communities, sit down with everyone that has input, and talk. Pool your knowledge regarding your loved one and check the boxes in your "needs" list. Once you have the "needs list" boxes checked, talk about the "wants list".

Once you have your top communities, now it is time to get to know them a little better. If you set up an appointment to visit the communities, assume that what you saw was their "Sunday best". The marketing representative probably walked the community before hand and made sure everything smelled okay, that the trash was picked up, etc. There are a couple things that you can do to see the "real" life community.

Drop by unannounced or show up on a weekend. Most communities have real life people that manage it. That means most of them work Monday through Friday. The better communities have a "Manager on Duty" where the senior managers take turns working one day or both days during the weekend. Their hours are usually somewhat abbreviated, but the purpose is both to make sure there is someone on site to address concerns, and to make sure that the staff comply with their standard operating procedure and to prevent the "while the cats away the mice will play" syndrome. This is a great time to drop by for an activity.

Show up on a weekend for a bingo game. This works great if you have time. If you have to find a place for your loved one before the weekend, then show up in the evening, around 6pm. This will be at the tail end of the dinner hour and usually when staffing levels are what they will be until after most residents are in bed.

The conduct of the staff after management is gone is a huge indicator of what kind of care your loved one will receive on the weekends, or the remaining 128 hours per week.

If you see something you do not like, bring it up to your marketing representative...then move on to the other communities in your final list.

# Chapter 10

## Let's talk $$$

This may be obvious to some, but it bears mentioning. When I have a potential resident and their family sitting in front of me, discussing how expensive the community is and how it will really stretch their budget, but it is "just doable"…it makes me cringe. Too often people focus on only the apartment rate. Depending on the community schedule of fees, that may be all they need to look at. Very few communities are "all inclusive". Therefore make sure you understand all the expenses for the community.

Ask basic financial questions when you visit the Assisted Living to capture the costs such as:

Is there a deposit (community fee)?

What charges are there if your loved one is sick and asks for meals to be delivered to their apartment? What charges are there for medication assistance? What are the charges for levels of care? That should all be clearly explained to you. If you run into a community that cannot clearly explain what is included in each service level, etc…walk away.

Other charges that may not be readily apparent, are pet and transportation charges. Is there a deposit for pets or a monthly fee? Is there a charge if the staff have to walk or feed the pet? Do they have a complimentary distance for transportation that they will drive before charging, and what are their transportation hours and fees? If your loved one has regular appointments, such as a specialist, dialysis or even a club they belong to, make sure those appointments are within those operational hours, or there may be a premium or simply no service. Medicaid has their own transportation services that the resident does not pay for, but requires scheduling 3 days in advance.

Ancillary charges? Do they charge for activities? Are there transportation charges? Most communities have a list of ancillary charges. This is required by the State of Arizona. Ask them for a copy of that sheet.

*Ensure that you understand the total "real world" cost of the community. The apartment rate is usually just the beginning of that actual cost.*

# Chapter 11

## The Assessment

The assessment is an evaluation of the persons needs prior to move-in. This will determine what level of care will be charged, and whether the community can meet their needs. Be as candid as possible. If you attempt to hide any aspects of your loved ones needs, then you are putting everyone in a very dangerous situation. The staff will soon determine what they actually need. If you are hiding a condition that would disqualify them from residency, when the staff find out, you will have to move and start the process all over again and you'll spend more money on another round of community fees and moving expenses, not to mention the psychological effects of constant change on your loved one.

The assessment is also a great opportunity to evaluate the community's nurse. Ask them questions. If you do not get precise answers, walk away. Nurses are not taught the basics of AL nursing in nursing school. The common practice is to assume that nurses with a skilled nursing background is well prepared for AL nursing. Unfortunately, this is not always the case. AL nursing requires management expertise. The nurse is generally in charge of supervising and training care staff, meeting state law, company policies as well as clinical support of their residents. The credentials of a nurse is less important (RN or LPN) than their organization and dedication. The community nurse will require support from their company and their resident's families. Most AL nursing is repetitive tracking of conditions. They are technicians, but not in the sense of an operating room nurse. They do not need to be experts in wound care or rehabilitation, but if their experience is years or decades in AL, you probably have a good nurse. Ask for their card and after the assessment (or preferably before) check their license with the state board of nursing. If there are derogatory actions taken, ask them to explain them.

The assessment should be in your loved one's current home. A good nurse or manager can glean quite a bit of information from where they live. Don't go in a day ahead of time and completely scrub the place down and clean it up. A disheveled house with mismatched items and medications strewn about the place are very important clues to understanding them.

Do not attempt to hide any behavioral issues. I have seen this many, many times and it usually ends up in a serious injury to another resident and a messy, expensive lawsuit afterwards. If dad gets upset and likes to punch people or mom likes to run people down with her walker, then the facility needs to know.

Medical issues are not the only things to mention during the contract. Family dynamics should be discussed and integrated into the Service Plan.

### Case Study: The prodigal son

I received a call one evening that a man was walking up and down the halls of our AL asking staff to witness a notarized document. The staff challenged the man and he said he was the resident's son. While the staff were on the phone with me, the son found a carpet crew working downstairs and had one of the men sign the document, which turned out to be several documents; POA, Healthcare POA, Financial POA and even a will.

The resident was moved into our facility by her daughter and second son who were well respected members of the community (a school principal and a senior police officer). I was completely unaware of the second son who turned out to be an adopted son that has had no contact with the family in nearly 20 years. The adopted son was ordered to leave the community by the staff.

I called the police the next day, and the detective that called back knew the adopted son by name. He was a known embezzler and had recently filed several lawsuits against the residents' biological children as well as Adult Protective Services complaints alleging that they had stolen his mother's money over the last 20 years.

The next night, while the daughter and son were visiting, the adopted son also visited. An argument ensued that nearly came to an all-out brawl...which is completely unacceptable in any Assisted Living. Again, the police were called and the responding officer was completely confused when he was presented with two different POA's.

Needless to say, had the facility been made aware of the family dynamic then we would have been better positioned to maintain our focus on the resident's care as opposed to nearly embroiling ourselves in a family dispute.

# Chapter 12

## The Contract

Once the assessment is complete and the decision has been made, the community will prepare a Residency Agreement. This is essentially a lease. Make sure any incentives are explained and included in writing and review the contract in detail with the community representative or ask for a copy to take home to review. If the community representative cannot explain each section of the contract, then do not sign it. Ask for clarification and follow-up.

Make sure you understand the grievance procedure and the community rules.

Make sure you understand how to terminate the agreement (usually a 30-day notice except for Medicaid).

Make sure that any addendums (for power chairs, pets, etc) are completely explained.

If something is not acceptable, ask for the document to be revised.

Also, ensure that you bring licensing and vaccination records for any pets to the contract signing.

### Case Study: Firepower

I had a WWII vet apply for residency at one of my communities. He was also a retired police officer. He was having trouble finding a community that would allow him to keep his prized war trophies and his service revolver.

After some discussion, we finally came to an agreement. Both the WWII rifle and his police revolver could be kept in his apartment in his display case, however, they would need to be certified as "disabled" by a gunsmith. This turned out to be a very simple process of removing the firing pin from the rifle, and a very specific spring from the revolver. Both solutions would make the firearms able to be restored to full function without destroying their value as rare collector items. The locked case was also required to reduce the likelihood of theft, and finally a Negotiated Risk Agreement was drafted and agreed to by all parties (at the request of our corporate legal department).

In that case, the rules were still met, but we as a community were willing to make a compromise to our "no weapons" policy in order to allow the resident to maintain two of his prize possessions and symbols of his identity.

**Resident Rights**

*Understand Resident Rights. Residents are not prisoners. If the community puts unreasonable restrictions on its residents, you can expect other "informal rules". Likely this is from a liability standpoint. Determine what is acceptable to you.*

# Chapter 13

## Move-in

I cannot say this enough. DO NOT BRING VALUABLES! They will disappear. Take the temptation away. Is there is a specific piece that mom or dad cannot live without? An heirloom watch, wedding band or collectible? If so, ask the staff to check it daily to ensure it is present and renters insurance is usually a very inexpensive option to cover non-sentimental items such as TV's, radios, furniture and small appliances. Make a list of items you moved in.

Make sure you do not overcrowd the apartment and consult with the nurse if you are unsure if a particular item is appropriate. As a manager, I would not allow rugs in the building. I have seen more falls from trips on rugs than from any other source.

Label clothes and belongings. A small sticker on the bottom of furniture, or a magic marker on the tag of clothing or a custom tag sewn into the collar or waistband.

Check with the maintenance director to determine what phone, internet and TV services are available. Find out ahead of time if you are permitted to hang pictures or TV's on walls or if their maintenance team must do it. Is there a fee to do so?

Make a day of the move-in just as you would with any other move. Stay for lunch or dinner and make sure mom or dad gets unpacked.

Introduce yourself to the staff and other family members. This will help with better communication in the future.

# Chapter 14

## Adjustment period

### The Service Plan or ISP

Before, during or shortly after move-in there should be a time to sit down with the staff of the facility to review the Service Plan, sometimes referred to as the Individual Service Plan. The Service Plan is the detailed instructions to the staff regarding what will be done for the resident. Everything from preferences to needs will be addressed.

This is the single most important document with regards to how well your loved one will be cared for. Ensure you review each section and fully understand what the community will be providing and what expectations there are on other entities. Will the facility or family be ordering medications? Is there a Case Manager that will be responsible for coordinating any services or transportation?

The caregivers will use the Service Plan as their guide. The expectations of what they will provide are detailed within that document. If it is not specifically mentioned in the Service Plan, DO NOT EXPECT IT TO HAPPEN. Some nurses and AL Managers are very, very good at creating service plans...some are not. The quality of the Service Plan will determine how smoothly the transition into AL will be as well as the quality of the care they will receive.

The Service Plan can be likened to a biography of the person's life and needs. The staff should be able to read this prior to meeting the resident and have a very good idea who they are and how to meet their needs. Details are extremely important and for each of these ADL's, these are some common things the nurse will need to know:

**Grooming:** Will staff brush the resident's teeth? Do they have dentures? Do they need assistance with brushing or putting toothpaste on the toothbrush? Do they brush their hair daily? What about shaving? Some men do not shave everyday so frequency and days are good to know. Do they put their hair in rollers at night? How do they get ready for bed? Do they simply wash their face with a warm wash cloth or is there a routine? Do they have a specific place they put their dentures when they take them out?

**Dressing:** Can they pick out clothes themselves? Do they need help with buttons or zippers? Is there a specific outfit they like to wear? Do they wear specific outfits on certain days? Do they need to change frequently (such as after meals). Do they layers clothes? Do they have assistive devices for dressing (such as shoe horns)? Do they put dirty clothes back on after wearing them?

**Bathing:** How often do they typically take a bath or a shower? What time of the day do they prefer to bathe? Do they use a shower chair? Do they like hot-hot water, warm water or cool water? Do they need assistance with any part of bathing (washing their hair, etc)? Where do they get their beauty supplies from? Do they have any soap allergies?

**Transfers:** Do they need assistance to stand up or switch from a wheelchair to a chair? Do they have any weakness on either side? Do they have a "trick knee"?

**Stability:** Do they get tired and unsteady after walking a few steps? Do they shuffle their feet? Have they fallen frequently?

**Medications:** Do they take their medications (pills) one at a time or all at once? Do they need their pills crushed and mixed in applesauce, yogurt or something else? Do they have a particular drink they take medications with? Do they need a lot of fluid to swallow them all?

## Caregivers: What to expect

In my opinion, nurses and caregivers are the hardest working staff in the facility. They are constantly pulled in different directions. Caregivers especially have a lot of expectations placed upon them.

Some caregivers are great...some should never be allowed around seniors. Get to know the caregivers. Ideally the same group of caregivers will work with your loved one daily. Although the same caregiver cannot work every single day, there should be some consistency.

Do not expect perfection. I hear constantly from families that "We took better care of mom at home." I do not doubt that, but you also have had 30-60 years to get to know them. The caregivers have to cram everything on that Service Plan into their day and integrate that into what they are doing for their other residents.

## Waiting period?

I often hear that facilities recommend against visiting for 7 to 14 days in order to allow the resident to adjust to the staff and their new surroundings. The idea is that they will have to learn to accept their new way of life.

I could not disagree more (except in some cases residents with dementia or Alzheimers moving into a memory care, but each resident's journey is different when encountering new places).

The idea is to demonstrate that their new life in an AL is not a prison, or a significant change from their old life. The resident should still be able to do the things they enjoyed previously such as going to lunch with friends, having grandchildren visit or even going shopping. If you isolate them for several weeks, they will likely resent moving into the AL and this will make their transition much more difficult.

**Expect some speed bumps**

One of my favorite quotes is "The perfect Assisted Living has yet to be invented". Nothing is perfect. Even the most well-oiled teams have things that go wrong. Some are preventable, some are unavoidable. Assume the best intentions and work with the community, physicians, case workers and social workers to get things done.

# Chapter 15

## Constant Contact

Make sure you build a good relationship with the nurse, manager and caregiver. Don't forget a token of appreciation around the holidays. Whether it is a bottle of wine or a gift card. Most companies have policies against this, but do it anyway. Caregivers are almost criminally underpaid and the nurses do not make much compared to other industries.

Keep an eye out for their comment cards and use them. Praise staff that do good things, and voice your concerns about others. Management cannot be everywhere.

You should see your relationship with the community as a partnership. Be active in service plan meetings and changes.

Again, assume the best intentions. People make mistakes. If you are one of those people that walk around with lawyers on your speed dial then this section is irrelevant to you. If you are not looking for a winning lottery ticket at your loved ones expense, then keep reading. There are many factors that contribute to illness and injury in a healthcare facility. Sometimes it is blatant neglect, but more often than not it is due to the workload common in today's healthcare system and the resident, family, physicians and caregivers share blame.

Most misunderstandings or conflict between communities happen when there is a breakdown in communication. The best way to fulfill your part of the partnership is to stay abreast of care and health changes as they are reported to you by the AL staff.

You will always know your loved one more than the AL staff possibly could. If there is an issue that arises, there is a good chance the staff will need your help to address it and when you were made the resident's guardian or POA, you assumed that responsibility.

# Chapter 16

## Changes in level of care

Inevitably at some point, your loved one will require more help and services. You should have drawn the conclusion that changes in needed care and services usually results in increased cost. If you moved into a community that pushes the budget when the resident moved in, likely they will not be able to afford the increased cost as needs increase. AL is a business and it does take more staffing hours and resources to take care of someone that needs more help. The increase in levels of care should be designed around this. Flat rate communities are great, but it also means you are paying for others care. The demands placed on the staff to meet other resident's needs will factor into what they are able to provide for your resident.

Review the suggested changes in level of care when they are presented and try to ignore the money aspect. If there is an issue with the increased cost of care indicated by the care staff, the nurse is not the person to argue with. You do not want a nurse that is willing to sacrifice quality of care for cost. The person you need to speak with is the AL Manager. Discuss the cost, but do not cut needed services. That puts the resident in a bad situation, and any responsible AL will likely terminate the residency agreement due to liability purposes and refer the resident to a community that can meet the resident's needs within their budget.

### Case Studies: I'm not paying for that!

While most states' regulations state that a resident is allowed to refuse any services they choose, this compromises the nurse's license as well as the AL Manager's license and presents a huge liability to the company.

I've run across several families that refused services due to cost. In one case, the family would not pay for medication management and spent a lot of their time trying to disprove our staff's observations.

In that particular case, the family representative was too busy to show up each night (as they promised) to check to make sure their mother had taken their medications. Their mothers' blood pressure dropped and the staff were not able to give her the requested medications because we did not have appropriate physicians orders. We had no idea if the medications were the correct dose or even the right drug. If we were to intervene, then we could have potentially done more harm. The only thing we could do is send the resident to the hospital each time. That resulted in much, much more money that the few hundred dollars a month the medication management would have cost.

In another case, the family refused to pay for a higher level of care that resulted from the residents' need for assistance with showering. The community could not allow the resident to take that high of a risk because they are responsible for the resident's safety. Therefore the community only had two choices;

One, the community could provide the services free of charge. That meant that the caregiver providing that service is not able to provide services to residents actually paying for their services. That is not fair to those paying residents.

Two, we could terminate their residency and they could find a community that could provide the required assistance at a rate the family could afford.

Believe it or not, option Two was best for the resident. By living in a community they could not afford, they would not receive the same quality of care as they would at a community which provided the services within their budget.

# Chapter 17

## Get on with your lives.

I don't mean "dump 'em and leave 'em", I mean get used to thinking of the place as their home. Visit, invite them out and get to know their neighbors. Recommend the community to others. Some communities will even give a bonus to family/friends for referrals. Go to the community events with your loved one and get to know their neighbors and friends. Don't think of their new home as a "facility", and do not hesitate to take them on day outings or spend the day with them.

Enjoy your time with them, and do not forget to take care of the caregiver (that's you). Taking care of yourself will give you the opportunity to enjoy your loved one rather than resenting them for the "burden" placed upon you. If you work well with their community, it will become less of a burden and you will have plenty of time to enjoy time spent with your loved one.

I hope this short guide was useful to you. I have answered these questions over and over during the course of my career and I have always found that the better informed or prepared an individual is, the less stressful the process is and the more likely it is for them to find a community that is the best fit for them.

Those of us who choose to work in this field do not hope for, nor receive, vast amounts of money. We chose the field because it is one of the most noble fields in healthcare, and unfortunately one of the least respected.

If you have any suggestions for information to be included in this book, please feel free to email me at jpayersbooks@gmail.com. If you would like various forms and checklists that will assist you with staying organized while searching for a community, I can email them to you in Word format so you can modify and print them as you see fit.

Please remember to leave feedback with the vendor you purchased or received this book so others can find and benefit from the book.

## About the authors

Jerrod Ayers, ALM/MBA is an industry professional and a certified Assisted Living Manager in the state of Arizona. He has been the Executive Director of a CCRC (IL/AL/MC/SNF/BH), several Assisted Livings and managed group homes from supervisory to directed memory care. He has held positions as the Accounting Manager for a CCRC, as community Human Resources and Marketing. Jerrod is currently the General Manager for The Oaks, a Merrill Gardens Community in Gilbert, AZ.

Nicole Walker, LPN is a seasoned Assisted Living Wellness Nurse. Her first job in healthcare was as a CNA in a traumatic brain injury facility in the Texas Hill Country. She has been an ER Nurse in a major metropolitan hospital as well as working for a national leader in fertility. Nicole chose to focus on Assisted Living as she felt that the industry was not given enough attention from the healthcare industry and has made it her focus to improve current systems, methodologies and to improve the quality of life for our seniors. Nicole is currently an Assisted Living

Supervisor for The Groves, a Merrill Gardens Community in Goodyear, AZ.

Jerrod and Nicole are married and have two beautiful daughters that share their home with them in Mesa, AZ.

www.ingramcontent.com/pod-product-compliance
Lightning Source LLC
Chambersburg PA
CBHW071102290526
45795CB00004B/1623